Lucy Maud
Montgomery

Terry Barber

MAPLE LEAF
SERIES

Lucy Maud Montgomery is published by
Grass Roots Press, a division of Literacy Services of Canada Ltd.

PHONE 1–888–303–3213
WEBSITE www.grassrootsbooks.net

ACKNOWLEDGMENTS

We acknowledge the financial support of the Government of Canada through the Canada Book Fund (CBF) for our publishing activities.

Produced with the assistance of
the Government of Alberta, Alberta
Multimedia Development Fund.

**Government
of Alberta ■**

Editor: Dr. Pat Campbell
Image research: Dr. Pat Campbell
Book design: Lara Minja

Library and Archives Canada Cataloguing in Publication

Barber, Terry, date
    Lucy Maud Montgomery / Terry Barber.

(Maple leaf series)
ISBN 978–1–926583–42–6

    1. Montgomery, L. M. (Lucy Maud), 1874–1942.
2. Novelists, Canadian (English)—20th century—Biography.
3. Readers for new literates. I. Title. II. Series: Barber, Terry, 1950– . Maple leaf series.

PE1126.N43B36517 2011   428.6'2   C2011–904443–9

Printed in Canada

Contents

but - he finally agreed.

So here I am in rather a plight. I've taken to a sheet of paper and written this highly graceful statement-

"You have a little more brains than the other Cavendish boys and I like brains - so I suppose I like you best - though I don't see why I should, after the trick you played you have played on us."

If Nate likes me best - I'd give him that- and he may take all the comfort- he can get out- of it. If he doesn't I'll tear it up and write Jack's name - true or not- true! "Desperate diseases require desperate remedies."

Besides, it will be true. If Nate says he likes anybody else best- I'll hate him!

Maud's journal.
1890

Maud's First Novel

Maud loves to write. She writes
whenever she can. Maud writes
poems. Maud writes stories. Then
Maud writes a **novel**. She wonders,
"Will my novel ever get published?"

Maud is
born in Prince
Edward Island
(P.E.I.).

Anne of Green Gables.

Maud's First Novel

Maud's novel is published. The novel is called <u>Anne of Green Gables</u>. The story is about a 12-year-old **orphan**. Maud is happy. She is also in for a surprise. Her novel sells thousands of copies. Maud becomes famous.

In the novel, Green Gables is a farm house in P.E.I.

Clara,
the mother of Maud.

Hugh John,
the father of Maud.

Early Years

Maud is born in 1874. Maud's mother dies when Maud is 21 months old. Her mother dies from **TB**. Maud's father goes west to find work. Maud must live with her grandparents. They are strict and religious. They read the Bible every night.

Maud's birthplace.

There are many books in Maud's home.

Early Years

Maud's grandfather is a good storyteller. Maud learns to tell stories, too. She is very smart. She teaches herself to read. Maud loves to read and write. When Maud turns nine, she begins to write a **journal**.

Maud, age 9.

Maud and her grandparents.

Early Years

Maud's grandparents believe a woman's place is in the home. Maud believes this too. Yet, she wants a different life. She dreams of becoming a famous writer. She enters writing contests. Maud likes to write poems the most.

Maud gets a poem published at the age of 15.

Maud travels over 3,000 kilometres to see her father.

Early Years

In 1890, Maud goes to live with her
father. She is 15 years old. Maud is
excited. Maud has not seen her father
in years. Maud is starved for her
father's love. Her father lives so far
away. Maud takes the train from P.E.I.

Maud's
father lives in
Prince Albert.

Hugh John and Mary Ann on their wedding day.
1889

Early Years

Maud's father has a new wife and baby. Maud and her stepmother do not get along. The stepmother treats Maud like a maid. She makes Maud look after her baby. She also makes Maud clean the house. Maud is homesick.

Maud returns to P.E.I. in 1891.

Maud gets her teaching certificate.
(Prince of Wales College, 1894)

The Teacher

Maud goes to college for one year.
In 1894, she gets her first teaching
job. She is only 19 years old. Maud

gets homesick.
She starts to
suffer from
mood swings.
Sometimes, she
gets depressed.
Sometimes,
she has a lot
of energy.

Maud, age 17.

Maud teaches school from 1896 to 1898.

The Teacher

Maud, age 22.

Maud gets up at 6 a.m. to write. She writes for an hour. Then she teaches school. Maud wants to become a better writer. In 1895, she goes to university for a year. Then, she runs out of money. Maud must start teaching again.

Ed is Maud's fiancé.

The Teacher

Maud teaches in a small community. She meets Ed. They get engaged. But she does not love Ed. She breaks up with him.

Maud falls in loves with Herman. He is a farmer. Maud feels Herman is beneath her. She turns her back on Herman.

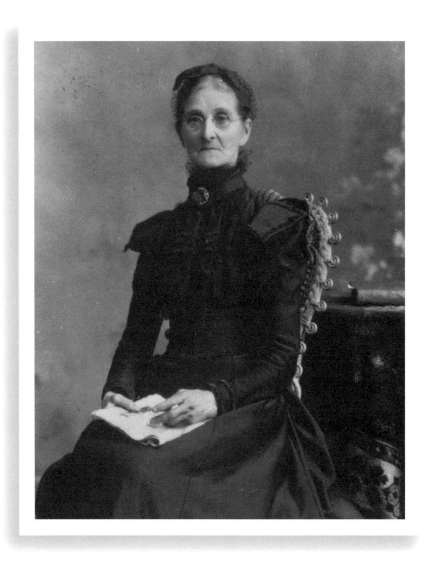

Maud's grandmother, Lucy MacNeill.

The Caregiver

In 1898, Maud's grandfather dies. Maud moves in with her grandmother. Maud's grandmother is a difficult woman. Maud feels trapped. She gets depressed again. But she has a strong sense of duty. Maud takes care of her grandmother for 13 years.

Maud's father dies in 1900.

Ewan Macdonald.

The Caregiver

In 1905, some light enters Maud's life. Maud meets a minister. His name is Ewan Macdonald. Ewan and Maud fall in love. They become engaged the next year. But they cannot marry. Maud must look after her grandmother.

Maud and Ewan are secretly engaged for 5 years.

Lucy Maud Montgomery, age 25.
1899

The Writer

Maud begins to earn money as a writer. Some of her poems and stories get published. Maud loves to see her name in print. Then, <u>Anne of Green Gables</u> is published. Maud is about to become famous.

Maud makes $73 from her writing in 1899.

Lucy Maud Montgomery, age 34.

The Writer

<u>Anne of Green Gables</u> is published in 1908. Readers love the novel. Reviewers love the novel. Maud's dream comes true. She is a famous writer. Maud's publisher wants more novels about Anne. Maud writes more "Anne" novels.

Maud is 34 years old when her novel is published.

Ewan and Lucy on their honeymoon.

The Wife and Mother

Maud's grandmother dies in 1911. Maud and Ewan marry the same year. Her marriage begins like a fairy tale. On their honeymoon, Maud and Ewan **tour** the British Isles. Maud loves to travel and visit new places.

Ewan's church in Leaskdale, Ontario.

The Wife and Mother

After their honeymoon, Maud and
Ewan leave P.E.I. Ewan takes a job in
Ontario. As a minister's wife, Maud
must be careful. Maud must not
gossip. But she likes to gossip. Maud
misses P.E.I.

Maud holds Stuart and Chester.
1917

The Wife and Mother

Maud and Ewan have three sons. Chester is born in 1912. The second son is born in 1914. He is **stillborn**. Maud's heart is broken. A third son, Stuart, is born in 1915.

Chester and Stuart.

This woman cuts oats in the field.

The Wife and Mother

Many men **enlist** in World War I. Now, women must do the work of men. Women run farms. Women work in factories. Women show they are strong. Women show they are smart. But they do not gain the same rights as men.

World War I starts in 1914 and ends in 1918. Over 600,000 Canadian men fight in the war.

Maud rests in her kitchen.

The Wife and Mother

Maud sees the world change. The years pass. Maud's marriage is less like a fairy tale. Ewan has health and mental problems. He cannot work. Maud suffers from depression. Her oldest son gets into trouble. For Maud, life is now a chore.

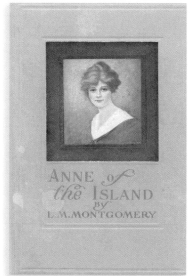

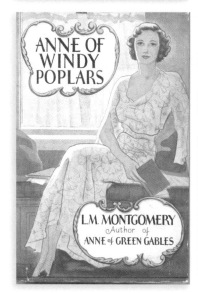

Maud writes 20 books.

Later Years

After the war, Maud's books become less popular. People want stories that are more real. Maud writes books with happy endings. But Maud keeps writing. She still makes a living as a writer. But she finds it harder to provide for her family.

Maud's grave in P.E.I.

Fame

Maud dies in April 1942. Today, her novels appear in many languages. People around the world love her stories. <u>Anne of Green Gables</u> becomes a TV series. Some of Maud's books become movies. Maud's fame lives on.

Maud published 20 novels and 500 poems and short stories.

Glossary

enlist: to join the Armed Forces as a volunteer.

feminist: a person who believes that women and men should have equal rights and opportunities.

journal: a daily record of personal experiences.

novel: a long made-up story.

orphan: a child whose parents are dead.

stillborn: born dead.

TB: tuberculosis is a lung disease.

tour: to take a trip from place to place.

Talking About the Book

What did you learn about Lucy Maud Montgomery?

What words would you use to describe Maud?

Do you think Maud was a **feminist**? Why or why not?

What hardships did Maud face in her life?

Do you think Maud was afraid of failure? Discuss.

How would you describe Maud's life?

Picture Credits

Front cover photos (center photo): © L.M. Montgomery Collection, Archival and Special Collections, University of Guelph; (small photo): © Ryrie-Campbell Collection, University of Prince Edward Island – Robertson Library/LM Montgomery Institute. Contents page (top left): © L.M. Montgomery Collection, Archival and Special Collections, University of Guelph; (bottom left): © Glenbow Archives NC-43-13; (bottom right): L.M. Montgomery Collection, Archival and Special Collections, University of Guelph. Page 6: *A Splendid Day,* by Ben Stahl, courtesy of Heirs of L. M. Montgomery Inc. Page 38: © Glenbow Archives NC-43-13. Page 42: © Ryrie-Campbell Collection, University of Prince Edward Island – Robertson Library/LM Montgomery Institute. All other photographs on pages 4 to 44: © L.M. Montgomery Collection, Archival and Special Collections, University of Guelph.